VIEWPOINTS ON
THE BOSTON
TEA PARTY

★ PART OF THE PERSPECTIVES LIBRARY ★

KRISTIN J. RUSSO

Published in the United States of America by Cherry Lake Publishing
Ann Arbor, Michigan
www.cherrylakepublishing.com

Reading Adviser: Marla Conn MS, Ed., Literacy specialist, Read-Ability, Inc.

Photo Credits: ©Wikimedia, cover (left), cover (middle); ©Grafissimo/iStockphoto/Getty Images, cover (right); ©Wikimedia, 1 (left), 1 (middle); ©Grafissimo/iStockphoto/Getty Images, 1 (right); ©Wikimedia, 4; ©duncan1890/Getty Images, 7; ©Wikimedia, 9; ©akg-images/Newscom, 10; © National Trust/ Wikimedia, 13; ©Jerry Tavin/Everett Collection/Newscom, 14; ©duncan1890/Getty Images, 16; ©Wikimedia, 18; ©Wikimedia, 19; ©The Print Collector / Heritage-Images/Newscom, 20; ©bauhaus1000/Getty Images, 22; ©duncan1890/Getty Images, 25; ©Wikimedia, 27; ©Wikimedia, 29; ©Grafissimo/iStockphoto/Getty Images, 32; ©duncan1890/Getty Images, 35; ©THEPALMER/Getty Images, 36; ©duncan1890/Getty Images, 38; ©The Print Collector / Heritage-Images/Newscom, 42; ©traveler1116/Getty Images, 44; ©akg-images/Newscom, 45; ©Picture History/Newscom, 45; ©Jerry Tavin/Everett Collection/Newscom, 46

Library of Congress Cataloging-in-Publication Data has been filed and is available at catalog.loc.gov

Cherry Lake Publishing would like to acknowledge the work of The Partnership for 21st Century Learning.
Please visit *www.p21.org* for more information.

Printed in the United States of America
Corporate Graphics

TABLE OF CONTENTS

In this book, you will read about the Boston Tea Party from three perspectives. Each perspective is based on real things that happened to real people who lived in or near Boston in 1773. As you'll see, the same event can look different depending on one's point of view.

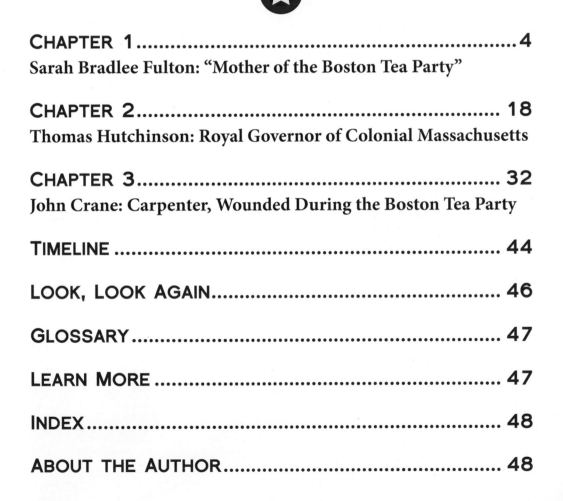

SARAH BRADLEE FULTON

"MOTHER OF THE BOSTON TEA PARTY"

It is hard work to keep the water at a low boil. I don't want to scald the men when they return, but I need the water to be hot enough to remove their face paint. Stirring the embers beneath the copper boiler should keep the water at a steady temperature without making it overheat. Sweat trickles down my neck from beneath my mobcap. My husband, John, will understand if I take a moment to step away from the fire and stretch my back. Though my chore is unpleasant, it is not half as difficult or as dangerous as that of my husband, my brother, and the nearly 60 other men with them.

My sister-in-law, Nathaniel's wife, is here to help me, but we can trust no one else with our secret. She wonders aloud how long it will be until the men return. The men have been gone for hours. I tell her that I think we shall see them soon.

I can't help it. An amused smile crosses my lips. My sister-in-law stifles a giggle. We are both thinking the same thing. John and Nathaniel and all of the others looked so odd when they left the house disguised as Native Americans. They prepared for their excursion to Boston Harbor by painting their faces and donning the type of clothing the Mohawk people wear. Their disguises were my idea.

While it made the men feel a bit silly, they did not

SECOND SOURCE

Find another source on the Stamp Act and compare the ifnormation provided there to the information in this source.

lose sight of the serious matter at hand. My husband, my brother, and the other **Sons of Liberty** plan to forcibly board and dump the contents of three English merchant ships anchored at Griffin's Wharf—the *Dartmouth*, the *Eleanor*, and the *Beaver*—into the Atlantic Ocean. Destroying this **cargo** is a **treasonous** crime and the consequences they face could be dire.

The English have only themselves to blame. Ever since the Stamp Act of 1765, troubles have been brewing between the colonists and the English. We colonists have never paid anything but local taxes. This we do not mind, as the funds pay for supplies and services we need right here in the colonies.

Then, King George III sent notice that he needed to raise funds to pay for the **Seven Years' War**. At his direction, **Parliament** enacted a new law called the

IN 1768, 4,000 BRITISH SOLDIERS WERE SENT TO BOSTON. THERE WERE ONLY 20,000 PEOPLE LIVING IN BOSTON AT THE TIME.

Stamp Act. Under this law, we were made to pay taxes on everything from wallpaper to newspapers to playing cards. All printed material had to have a special stamp to show that the **appropriate** taxes had been paid. Ridiculous!

THE SONS OF LIBERTY

John Adams, one of the most famous members of the Sons of Liberty, later became the first vice president of the United States and the nation's second president. He argued for the president to be known as "His Majesty the President," "Excellency," or "His Highness the President of the United States of America and Protector of the Rights of the Same." None of his ideas were adopted.

When Parliament repealed the controversial Stamp Act in 1766, they enacted a new law at the same time. The Declaratory Act gave Parliament the authority to pass new taxes on the colonists at any time.

PART OF THE STAMP ACT SAID THAT COLONISTS COULD BE TRIED FOR CRIMES WITHOUT A JURY. MANY PROTESTS ERUPTED OVER THIS ISSUE.

We understand that war costs money, and we are glad that England prevailed against the French, but we will not accept being made to follow laws that we have had no voice in enacting. While it is true that English soldiers provided protection for the colonists during the war, and still do, the fact is that we are being taxed without representation. There is no one in Parliament who represents the best interests of the colonists.

Naturally, we rebelled against the Stamp Act. We smuggled the goods we wanted or procured them through bartering. It was not long before Parliament admitted defeat and repealed the Stamp Act.

But the king's greed knows no bounds! He tried to tax us again through the Townshend Acts. These laws placed taxes on glassware and chinaware—even paint! How funny that the men are using paint tonight to rebel against these injustices.

With **boycotts** and protests, we have overcome

all but one of these unfair laws—the Tea Act. This law requires us to buy all of our tea from the **East India Company**. The East India Company is a large business, and the economy in England relies on its success, so Parliament has stepped in to save this failing company—on our backs! We can buy tea for less money from the French and the Dutch, but this new law will not allow us to be economical with our household funds. And of course, the East India Company is an English company, and so all of the profit will go to English merchants, who pay taxes to the king. This is a sneaky way of taxing the colonists.

We have had enough of unjust laws and "taxation without representation." One law is repealed only to be replaced with another. It is causing chaos in our lives. Well, we can cause chaos too.

My sister-in-law signals to me that she thinks she can hear the men arriving. Of course they are

THE TOWNSHEND ACTS WERE NAMED FOR
CHARLES TOWNSHEND, WHO HELD A POSITION IN
THE BRITISH GOVERNMENT SIMILAR TO THE
U.S. TREASURER.

THE BOSTON TEA PARTY WAS NOT CALLED BY THAT
NAME UNTIL 1825.

being as quiet as possible! They must not get caught!

But if all went as planned, the men have just dumped

342 chests of tea into Boston Harbor.

John and Nathaniel and a handful of men enter

as quietly as possible. John catches my eye and nods

to me. The deed is done! Quickly and silently, my sister-in-law and I set about helping the men clean the paint from their faces and dispose of their Mohawk garb. We are careful not to burn their faces with the warm water, but all the paint must be removed.

Later, when all the evidence of the crime is hidden and all the men have dispersed to their homes, John tells me something that pleases me, something he overheard Samuel Adams say. Samuel Adams is the leader of the Sons of Liberty. He is an important patriot. "With ladies on our side, we can make the **Tories** tremble," he said.

The Tories support the king and stand by his right to rule, no matter how greedy he is. Even in our own neighborhoods there are Tories who are loyal to the king. They are willing to sell

THINK ABOUT IT

Determine the main point of this paragraph and pick out one piece of evidence that supports it.

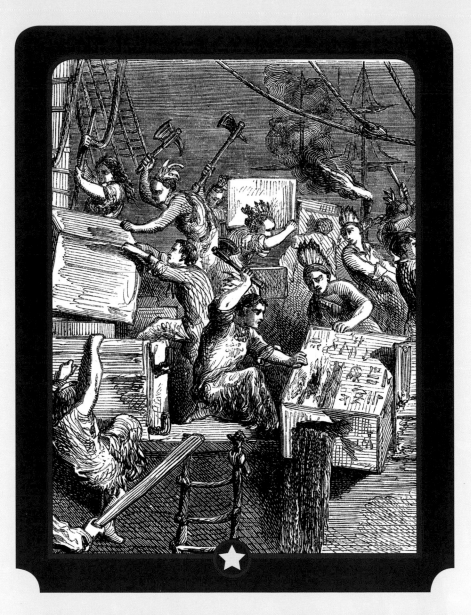

THE COLONISTS WERE NOT TRYING TO STEAL THE
TEA, THEY WERE FOCUSED ON DESTROYING IT SO
IT COULD NOT BE SOLD.

British goods and force the taxes upon us. Sometimes the loyalists are easy to spot. But sometimes it is impossible to tell who they are. There is treachery everywhere, among family and long-held friendships. That is why we must keep our involvement in tonight's "tea party" a secret. It is difficult to figure out who supports the king's unfair laws and who supports the colonists' efforts to resist.

I am proud of my role in helping to overcome English tyranny, but I have a sinking feeling that our troubles have just begun.

THOMAS HUTCHINSON

ROYAL GOVERNOR OF COLONIAL MASSACHUSETTS

Samuel Adams is the bane of my existence and has been ever since we were young men. Years ago, in 1740 and 1741, Samuel Adams's father tried to operate a new kind of bank that used land and property as the basis for money instead of silver and gold. This decreased the use of British notes and coins. Naturally, the king had to be told, and so I, as a selectman of Boston, wrote to

Parliament about the whole business. Just as I suspected, Parliament declared all land banks to be illegal and ordered them to be shut down.

GOVERNOR THOMAS HUTCHINSON'S BOSTON MANSION WAS DESTROYED ON AUGUST 26, 1765, WHEN RIOTERS BROKE THE FRONT DOOR WITH AN AX AND TOOK VALUABLE ITEMS, INCLUDING CLOTHING, SILVER, AND PAINTINGS.

WHILE HUTCHINSON FLED FOR HIS LIFE, RIOTERS AT HIS HOME DESTROYED EVERYTHING HE OWNED, INCLUDING A LIBRARY OF BOOKS IT HAD TAKEN HIM 30 YEARS TO COLLECT.

It's not my fault the business ended in his financial ruin. The Adams family should never have started the bank in the first place. Adams is also angered that I insisted that his own tax debt be paid.

After his father's death, he had been elected tax collector, and it was his job to collect taxes from the townspeople. If they did not pay, that debt became his own. I did not make this rule, but it was my duty as lieutenant governor at the time to see that it was followed. As a representative of the Crown, I had to insist that he take responsibility for the taxes his friends would or could not pay. Now he blames me for his financial hardships and has set his Sons of Liberty upon me like a plague.

For years while I served as lieutenant governor, and now that I have been named royal governor, Samuel Adams has sabotaged my rule with mischief, lies, and vandalism. First, he and his men, the Sons of Liberty, threatened merchants who sold British goods. They broke into their shops and destroyed their property. And they encouraged the colonists to boycott British goods. The Sons of Liberty also interfered with the Townshend Acts, vandalizing

SAMUEL ADAMS, A FOUNDING MEMBER OF THE
SONS OF LIBERTY, ONCE SAID, " "IT DOES NOT
TAKE A MAJORITY TO PREVAIL . . . BUT RATHER AN
IRATE, TIRELESS MINORITY, KEEN ON SETTING
BRUSHFIRES OF FREEDOM IN THE MINDS OF MEN."

stores that sold British goods and tar and feathering loyalist merchants. Again, Parliament backed down, repealing the Townshend Acts but leaving one tax in place—a measly three pence per pound tax on tea.

Three pence! Any sensible person could see that this is a reasonable amount. Where do they think the money comes from that is used to protect them from the French? From the Native Americans? The Seven Years' War ended 10 years ago. Its costs must be paid. The funds come from taxes, of course. These colonists do not even realize when laws are enacted that are good for them. Instead, they resist, refusing to buy British tea and drinking a bitter concoction made from native plants instead.

Parliament has backed down enough already, first by repealing the Stamp Act and then by repealing the Townshend Acts. The Tea Act will remain, I am sure of it. Parliament will not show weakness again. In fact, it has sent three merchant ships to Boston under the protection of British warships, the *Dartmouth*, the *Beaver*, and the *Eleanor*. They are anchored at Griffin's Wharf. Adams and his men are calling for me to send the ships back to England, but I will stand my ground. The ships will stay, and the customs taxes will be paid.

Day and night the Sons of Liberty watch over the merchant ships. They hold about 90,000 pounds (40,000 kilograms)—more than 300 chests—of tea from the East India Company. These ships have already entered Boston Harbor and have been boarded by port officials. This relieves the captains of their responsibility for their ships. They are my problem now.

There are local merchants here in Boston who are willing to sell the tea, even though it means paying customs taxes on it, but the Sons of Liberty will not allow the cargo to be unloaded. They oppose all taxes owed to the Crown, no matter how small.

Their actions are unreasonable, but I am unwilling

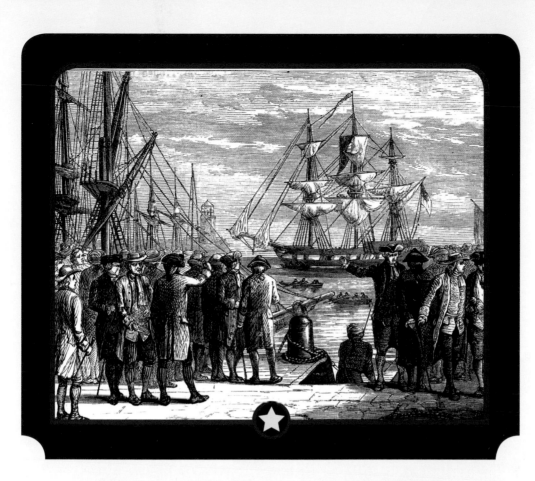

**THE EAST INDIA COMPANY TEA ABOARD THE
DARTMOUTH IN BOSTON HARBOR WAS ACTUALLY
IMPORTED FROM CHINA.**

to make any move that could prompt violence. We
have had enough of that already. The mood among the
colonists is still angry and distrustful three years after
the Bloody Massacre in King Street. Even this they
blame on me, when it was clearly the colonists' fault.

Several Bostonian colonists surrounded and threatened my soldiers. Fearing for their lives, they fired in self-defense and killed five locals. There is a rumor that Samuel Adams wrote stories for the newspaper that exaggerated the event. He is trying to impact public opinion in order to make the colonists' hatred of my British soldiers even worse. He is an uncouth man, untrustworthy and unkempt. Lying is not beneath him.

I admit that my nerves are more frazzled over this matter now that the ships have been moved closer together. The Sons of Liberty insisted on this. This makes me think that the men have something unseemly in mind. But perhaps it's just that they want it to be easier to keep an eye on the cargo. So far, all seems quite calm. The ships' captains have even left the vessels in the care

ANALYZE THIS

Analyze two of the perspectives on the Sons of Liberty in this book. How are they alike? How are they different?

THE BOSTON MASSACRE WAS NOT CALLED BY
THAT NAME UNTIL MANY YEARS AFTER IT HAPPENED.
AT FIRST, IT WAS CALLED THE "BLOODY MASSACRE
IN KING STREET." LATER, IT WAS ALSO CALLED THE
"STATE STREET MASSACRE."

of their first mates, and they are moving about freely in Boston, conducting business and waiting patiently for the matter to be resolved.

I do sense a measure of unease among the merchants who are willing to sell the tea, however. They are called "Tories" or "loyalists." They have begun to seek refuge with me at Castle William.

How right the loyalists are! I have just received

BOSTON MASSACRE

British soldiers had been brought to the colonies in 1768 to enforce the Townshend Acts. Tension between the soldiers and colonists was high. On March 5, 1770, a fight broke out when a mob surrounded a group of soldiers. The soldiers fired on the crowd and five colonists were killed.

CASTLE WILLIAM PROVIDED REFUGE TO GOVERNOR
HUTCHINSON AND OTHER LOYALISTS LEADING UP
TO THE AMERICAN REVOLUTIONARY WAR. TODAY, IT
IS OPEN TO VISITORS AND IS RUN BY THE
U.S. NATIONAL PARK SERVICE.

word that about 60 men, some disguised as Mohawk people and others simply camouflaged with coal dust and dark face paint, have made their way to Griffin's Wharf carrying hatchets. They joined the Sons of Liberty who were already there on watch and formed raiding parties with others who came from towns and villages outside of Boston.

SECOND SOURCE

Find an outside source on the Sons of Liberty and compare the information there to the information in this source.

Enough men arrived to make three raiding parties of about 50 each. They boarded the ships and dumped every single chest of tea into the ocean. Every single one. They were careful to leave the rest of the cargo undamaged, since it was not subject to the tea tax, but still, their actions are barbaric!

All the tea is destroyed, and not one penny in customs taxes has been paid. None of it was salvageable, and none of the colonists took any of it for themselves. They appear to be principled, but I think they are foolish.

The Sons of Liberty have made a grave error. I fear for them now. The king will be furious when he hears of their treason. I would not be surprised at all if Parliament passes laws that will make their lives intolerable. These unruly colonists certainly deserve it.

JOHN CRANE

CARPENTER, WOUNDED DURING THE BOSTON TEA PARTY

It is December 16, 1773. My house is full of men and my wife, Mehitable, has her hands full serving ale and helping us all into our disguises. We are due to meet with the other Sons of Liberty down at Griffin's Wharf at about six o'clock in the evening. Though our planned operation is top secret, dangerous even, I am looking forward to it. I am no stranger to combat.

I fought alongside the famous war general, George Washington, in the French and Indian War. The English call it the Seven Years' War, but we colonists know who the enemy was, and we call it like we see it.

I was only 12 then. You think that's too young to fight, don't you? Well, a man has to do what a man has to do. It was true for my father, and it was true for me, even at that tender age. My father was conscripted to fight against the French and Native Americans, but he was unable to leave the family homestead in Braintree, Massachusetts, and I went in his place. The English made us fight in their war, and now they want to tax us to pay for it? An insult! We shall not stand for it! It feels like a fight is brewing again, and I will be ready for it.

We are ready. In mid-December, it has already been dark for hours, even though it is early evening. We make our way quietly through the streets toward the wharf. I see no reason why we shouldn't make a complete spectacle of ourselves, even bring a fifer along. If we are to protest and resist, we should make our intent known!

Instead, we march toward this protest in near silence. We are about to commit a treasonous crime. But what choice do we have? The English will not lord their tyranny over us without loud resistance.

THINK ABOUT IT

Determine the main idea of this paragraph and pick out one piece of evidence that supports it.

The merchant ship, the *Dartmouth*, arrived in Boston on November 28. Since then, we have been greatly agitated by its presence and the two that followed shortly thereafter, the *Beaver* and the *Eleanor*. We have held several meetings at the Old South Meeting House to try to come to a decision about what to do. We will certainly not accept the tea that is on board, as it means paying the hated tea tax.

FANEUIL HALL IS ALSO KNOWN AS THE "CRADLE OF LIBERTY." IT IS LOCATED IN BOSTON.

The English argue that it is only 3 pence. Well, 3 pence is 3 pence. If a man earns his money, he has a right to keep it!

THE ROLE THAT SAMUEL ADAMS PLAYED IN THE
EXECUTION OF THE BOSTON TEA PARTY HAS NEVER
BEEN DETERMINED. THE SONS OF LIBERTY FOUNDER
REMAINED SECRETIVE ABOUT HIS INVOLVEMENT TO
AVOID ARREST.

We have even appealed to Governor Hutchinson, though the Sons of Liberty leader Samuel Adams has always found Hutchinson to be a petty and unreasonable man. Still, we presented our case

ANALYZE THIS

Analyze two of the accounts in this book that detail when the tea was thrown into the water. How are they alike? How are they different?

and appealed to the governor's sense of morality and duty toward the people of Boston. We told him that he should **expel** the ships from the harbor unloaded. In this way, we can avoid paying the customs tax. Hutchinson was unmoved. He noted that port authorities had already boarded the ships, and that meant the tax had to be paid. At our last meeting, the governor sent his final word. He is not on our side. He will not expel the ships. Therefore, we must expel their contents.

I think this is an excellent plan and am proud to be part of it. Quickly, the nearly 160 men assembled

Most of the participants in the Boston Tea Party were from Boston, but the event attracted protesters from as far away as Worcester, Massachusetts, and even Maine.

split into three groups. I stay with the men I have come with and we board one of the ships. It is dark and I am not certain which ship I have boarded, but I know what I must do.

One of the men asks the first mate for lanterns and for keys to the cargo hold. We explain that we are here to destroy only the tea, and that the other items on board will remain unharmed as long as the ship's mates do not interfere. In a civilized manner, the first mate provides the keys and lanterns. He is keen to save as much of the cargo as possible. He must answer to his captain when all is said and done.

I will bet he wonders why the British warships sent to protect these merchant ships refuse to interfere. I admit, I wonder about this myself. I had expected more of a fight. For some reason, Admiral Montagu and his Royal Navy sailors, who have been sent by the Crown to protect the merchant ships, do not intervene, though some of the sailors taunt us from afar. Their taunts are easy enough to ignore.

In the dim light, we set about our work. With hatchets in hand, we open the chests of tea and dump the contents into the ocean. We carry chest after chest of tea to the deck and heave them over the side. We work well together, but the work is difficult, and we must make sure we get it all without damaging the

THE INTOLERABLE ACTS

As punishment for the Boston Tea Party, the British Parliament passed five laws, which Bostonians called the Intolerable Acts. Under the acts, Boston Harbor was closed until the town paid for the destroyed tea. Boston was placed under military rule, and British troops could be **quartered** in the townspeople's homes without their consent.

ship or anything else. We must destroy 45 tons of tea this night. It is tedious and difficult work.

My muscles are sore. Face paint and sweat drips from my face. It is hot and stuffy below deck and as cold as ice aboveboard, but these difficult conditions will not deter me. As a young soldier, I faced circumstances that were far worse.

The last of the chests are deep in the cargo hold. I head down to grab another chest. Suddenly, I am hit in the head from behind, and all goes black.

After this, I remember nothing until I awake in a pile of wood shavings. I sputter and spew the shavings away from my mouth and nose. I still wear my Mohawk garb, and I am covered entirely by a pile of wood chips. How did I get here?

My first thought is of Mehitable. I can see through an open window that the sun is beginning to rise. She will worry that I did not return home before sunup. Though I am a carpenter and used to sawdust

MANY PEOPLE WHO PARTICIPATED IN THE BOSTON TEA PARTY KEPT THEIR IDENTITIES SECRET. ONLY 116 PEOPLE HAVE HAD THEIR PARTICIPATION DOCUMENTED, THOUGH MANY MORE WERE REPORTEDLY INVOLVED.

and the sweet smell of wood shavings, having them cover my nose and mouth causes me to cough and choke. With each cough, my head feels like it will split open. When I fight my way to the top of the pile, I breathe in deeply, grateful for the fresh air that fills my lungs.

How I long for Mehitable's help. She will bring me

a cold draft of ale and clean away the sticky paint and wood shavings. It takes a moment for my mind to clear before I realize where I am. I am at a carpenter's shop not far from the wharf. My journey home will be a short one, but I must make it on my own two feet. There is no one here to help me.

When I enter my home, Mehitable throws herself into my arms. My friends told her that I was dead, hit from behind by a falling chest of tea in a cargo hold deep inside the ship. My friends hid me in the pile of wood shavings at the carpenter's shop. They had planned to return for me later. Won't they be surprised when they return to find me missing? I would laugh at this if it were not for my splitting headache.

With tears of relief running down her cheeks, Mehitable helps me dispose of my disguise and puts me to bed to recover from my injury. A head wound is a small price to pay to protest the insults and chaos the English have thrust upon us.

TIMELINE

BOSTON TEA PARTY

Parliament passes the Tea Act. The tax on tea is lowered, but Parliament maintains its right to tax the colonists. They must pay all taxes that are imposed.

MAY 10,
1773

Seven loyalist merchants in Boston are chosen to sell tea provided by the East India Company.

AUGUST 4,
1773

The *Dartmouth* docks in Boston Harbor carrying tea from the East India Company. The *Beaver* and the *Eleanor* follow on December 2 and December 7. The Sons of Liberty appoint 25 men to guard the ships to make sure none of the tea is unloaded.

NOVEMBER 28,
1773

DECEMBER 13,
1773

Citizens of Lexington, Massachusetts, set a bonfire and burn all the tea they own.

DECEMBER 16,
1773

Francis Rotch, owner of the *Dartmouth*, reports that Governor Hutchinson will not give him permission to move his ship without unloading it.

DECEMBER 16,
1773

In disguise, the Sons of Liberty gather at Griffin's Wharf and throw 342 chests of tea from the three tea ships into the harbor.

LOOK, LOOK AGAIN

Take a close look at this illustration of the Boston Tea Party and answer the following questions:

1. What would the wife of a patriot see in this picture? What would she think of the men tossing the tea overboard? Would she see them as heroes or villains? Why?

2. How would the royal governor of Massachusetts describe this picture to the members of Parliament in England? What would the governor, who represents the Crown, think when looking at this scene?

3. What would a patriot notice and think about this scene? How would the patriot think differently from a loyalist about the men who tossed the tea?

GLOSSARY

appropriate *(app-PRO-pree-et)* especially suitable or compatible

boycotts *(BOI-cots)* refusing to buy, use, or participate in something as a way of protesting

cargo *(car-GO)* the goods or merchandise conveyed in a ship

East India Company *(EEST IN-dee-uh KUHM-puh-nee)* a British trading company

expel *(ex-PEL)* to force out

parliament *(PAR-le-ment)* an assemblage of the nobility, clergy, and commons called together by the British sovereign as the supreme legislative body in the United Kingdom

quartered *(KWOR-terd)* housed in a dwelling

Seven Years' War *(SEV-un YEERS WOR)* called the French and Indian War in the colonies, a war fought partly in America in which Austria, France, Sweden, and Russia fought Britain, Hanover, and Prussia for a number of territories

Sons of Liberty *(SUNZ UV lib-ur-TEE)* a secret group of patriots that protected and fought for the rights of colonists against the British government

Tories *(TOR-eez)* colonists who were loyal to the English government

treasonous *(TREE-zon-ous)* the offense of trying to overthrow a government to which a person owes allegiance

LEARN MORE

FURTHER READING

Brennan, Linda Crotta. *Boston Tea Party: A History Perspectives Book*. Ann Arbor, MI: Cherry Lake Publishing, 2014.

Murray, Stuart. *American Revolution*. New York: DK, 2015.

Tovar, Alicia. *The Boston Tea Party: No Taxation Without Representation*. New York: PowerKids Press, 2016.

WEBSITES

Boston 1774
http://www.pbs.org/ktca/liberty/chronicle_boston1774.html
This website describes what happened after the Boston Tea Party.

Boston Tea Party
http://www.masshist.org/revolution/teaparty.php
This website explains more about the Boston Tea Party and shows documents from the time period.

INDEX

ABOUT THE AUTHOR

Kristin J. Russo is a university English lecturer. She loves teaching, reading, writing, and learning new things. She and her husband live near Providence, Rhode Island, in a small house surrounded by flower gardens. They have three grown children and three rescue dogs.